INSPIRING LIVES

ROBERT JOHNSON

Legend of the Delta Blues

By James Patrick

Gareth Stevens
Publishing

Please visit our Web site www.garethstevens.com. For a free color catalog of all our high-quality books, call toll free 1-800-542-2595 or fax 1-877-542-2596.

Library of Congress Cataloging-in-Publication Data

Patrick, James.
 Robert Johnson : legend of the Delta blues / James Patrick.
   p. cm. — (Inspiring lives)
 Includes index.
 ISBN 978-1-4339-3620-3 (pbk.)
 ISBN 978-1-4339-3621-0 (6-pack)
 ISBN 978-1-4339-3619-7 (library binding)
 1. Johnson, Robert, d. 1938—Juvenile literature. 2. Blues musicians—United States—Biography—Juvenile literature. I. Title.
 ML3930.J585P37 2010
 782.421643092--dc22
 [B]
                              2009037271

Published in 2010 by Gareth Stevens Publishing
111 East 14th Street, Suite 349
New York, NY 10003

Copyright © 2010 Gareth Stevens Publishing

Designer: Michael Flynn
Editor: Therese Shea

Cover and p.1 (Robert Johnson), p. 5
Robert Johnson Studio Portrait
Hooks Bros., Memphis, 1935
© 1989 Delta Haze Corporation
All Rights Reserved; Used By Permission

Photo credits: Cover and p. 1 (background), pp. 9, 15, 23, 29 Shutterstock.com;
p. 7 © Hulton Archive/Getty Images; p. 11 © Bernard Hoffman/Time & Life Pictures/Getty Images; p. 13 © GAB Archive/Redferns/Getty Images; p. 17 © David E. Scherman/Time & Life Pictures/Getty Images; p. 19 © Fox Photos/Hulton Archive/Getty Images; p. 21 © Rita Weigand/Getty Images; p. 25 © Robert Knight/Redferns/Getty Images; p. 27 (Eric Clapton) © Mick Hutson/Redferns/Getty Images; p. 27 (Rolling Stones) © Chris McGrath/Getty Images.

Printed in the United States of America

CPSIA compliance information: Batch #CW10GS: For further information contact Gareth Stevens, New York, New York at 1-800-542-2595.

Contents

Meet Robert Johnson

Robert Johnson was a great musician. He played and wrote blues music.

Growing Up

Robert was born in Hazlehurst, Mississippi, in 1911. His family was poor. They worked on a farm.

MISSISSIPPI

Jackson ★

● Hazlehurst

Robert loved music. He learned to play the harmonica. Then he learned to play the guitar.

harmonica

guitar

9

Living the Blues

Robert married Virginia Travis in 1929.

She died in 1930. Their baby died, too.

Robert began to play the blues a lot.

Fast Learner

Robert listened to famous blues musicians Lonnie Johnson and Son House. He wanted to play like them.

Son House

13

Robert practiced a lot. He surprised people. They wondered how he learned so fast.

Sharing the Blues

Robert played in towns along the Mississippi River. The music he played was called Delta blues.

Mississippi River

Robert played in Chicago and Detroit, too. He even played on the radio.

Chicago, 1930

In Arkansas, Robert Johnson met a young man named Robert Lockwood Jr. He taught Robert Lockwood Jr. to play the blues.

Robert Lockwood Jr.

Robert Johnson began to record his songs in 1936. He recorded twenty-nine songs.

record player

23

The Music Lives On

Robert died in 1938. Some people think he was poisoned. He was only 27 years old.

ROBERT L. JOHNSON
MAY 8, 1911 ~ AUGUST 16, 1938
-musician & composer-
influenced millions beyond his time.

Nazareth. King of Jerusalem.
my Redeemer liveth and that
call me from the Grave.
JOHNSON, SHORTLY BEFORE HIS DEATH AND PRE
PAPERS BY HIS SISTER, CARRIE H. THOMPSON

Eric Clapton and the Rolling Stones play Robert's songs. Other musicians play them, too.

Eric Clapton

Rolling Stones

Robert Johnson is a member of the Rock and Roll Hall of Fame. He made many people love the blues.

Rock and Roll
Hall of Fame

1911 Robert is born in Hazlehurst, Mississippi.

1929 Robert marries.

1930 Robert's wife and child die.

1936 Robert begins to record songs.

1938 Robert dies.

1986 Robert is made a member of the Rock and Roll Hall of Fame.

For More Information

Books:

Koopmans, Andy. *The History of the Blues*. San Diego, CA: Lucent Books, 2005.

Lewis, J. Patrick. *Black Cat Bone: The Life of Blues Legend Robert Johnson*. Mankato, MN: Creative Editions, 2006.

Web Sites:

Robert Johnson Blues Foundation
www.robertjohnsonbluesfoundation.org

Rock and Roll Hall of Fame and Museum: Robert Johnson
www.rockhall.com/inductee/robert-johnson

Glossary

blues: a kind of sad music

delta: land shaped like a triangle at the mouth of a river. When spelled with a capital "D," it means the area around the Mississippi delta.

harmonica: a small musical instrument with holes that people blow into

musician: someone who plays or writes music

poisoned: having taken something into the body that causes illness or death

record: to make a copy of sound

Index